lebanon
THROUGH THE LENS OF MUNIR NASR

Credits:

Photography: Munir Nasr
Layout: Mireille Nasr Aoun

Text: Angélique Beaino
Editor: Henri Zoghaib

Special thanks to:

Ministry of tourism   - maps of touristic sites
                                 - interior photographs of the Lebanese National Museum

Mapas Co.   - Jeita Grotto

Also available in:
French
German
Spanish
Italian
Arabic

© Munir Nasr
Beirut P.O.Box 90-1970, Mobile: 00961-3-813450, Tel/Fax: 00961-1-680 488,
info@munirnasr.com   www.munirnasr.com

Printed in Lebanon by Arab Printing Press sal

ALL RIGHTS RESERVED
No photographs or part of this publication may be reproduced or transmitted in any form or by any means without a written permission from the copyrighter.

(Hard Cover): ISBN: 978-9953-0-2384-7   (Soft Cover): ISBN: 978-9953-0-2385-4

foreword

If it's not a new book on Lebanon, it's definitely a book with a new point of focus on Lebanon's outstanding views.

Munir Nasr, an affectionate Lebanese citizen and – how highly qualified – photographer, tries to share, with this book readers, major focal glimpses of his camera lens all around the country.

Munir Nasr

You will pass, throughout these pages, by the worldwide known and most beautiful (historical, religious and cultural) cities, sites and regions of Lebanon; you'll get provided with extraordinary discoveries about our ancient, very ancient country, as well as selected bouquets of panoramic photographs, revealing Lebanon's splendor and elegance. The majority of these aforementioned cities and regions have played an active and major role in Lebanon's history, and therefore have drawn the attention of many kings, scholars and writers since ancient times, who have brought an academic and scientific interest towards Lebanon, mainly those (e.g. Ernest Renan, Maurice Dunand, …) who wanted to unearth the glorious past of these cities, and the ones who may have the interest to deepen their knowledge about these mysterious Lebanon's cities, sites and regions.

This book aims, as well, at reviving images of past civilizations (fairly preserved by nature and man) along with the new modern Lebanon which, like its symbol the phoenix, resuscitated from its ashes to become a gem of vivid jewelry among the neighboring countries, with its new architecture, vivacity and role, beside being, mythically, a center of various millennium civilizations, cultures, religions, history, nature and myths that have since ever fascinated scholars, writers, and archeologists (e.g. Eusebius, Nonnos, Lamartine, Renan, Dunand, …).

Having conceived this book not as a simple regular guide, but rather as a companion of the tourists and scholars, Munir Nasr has caught through his camera lens the most charming sites and enchanting views of Lebanon's nature and beauty, which are masterfully depicted in the texts of Angélique Béaino.

Who else could have professionally achieved such a highly perfect job, he who worked (as a photographer for more than twenty years) for the United Nations in Vienna-Austria, visiting and photographing various subjects in many countries. His photographs were permanently exhibited at the Vienna International Center, part of his work was exhibited at the UN Headquarters in New York. Nasr was awarded numerous international and local prizes as well.

Upon his final return to Lebanon, he started to frame the moments and shoot new photographs to rebuild his photo library after having lost all his works during the war in Lebanon. He has always kept, during his diasporas travels, the will of publishing a book joining, by photos and words, the important and beautiful cities, villages and mountains of Lebanon, to be kept in every library in Lebanon and abroad.

His passion for this art was transferred to his children, of whom Mireille who grew up, studied and graduated in Vienna. She mingled the photographs and texts in the artistic lay out of the present book.

Upon the second edition of the book, many regions have been added, allowing the tourists to discover new natural sceneries and villages.

May each and every one who gets this book, find - within its photos and texts - a glimpse of this beautiful Lebanon, this real gift heavenly given to the Lebanese and their appreciating ones.

Henri Zoghaib

history

Lebanon is a small country, just 10,452 square kilometers, situated at the crossroads of three continents: Europe, Asia and Africa. It is the historic home of the Phoenicians, Semitic traders whose maritime culture flourished for more than two thousand years (circa 2700-450 B.C.).

Lebanon's rich heritage and special charm have attracted travelers, tourists and conquerors throughout the ages. At different periods in its history, it has been ruled by the Assyrians, Babylonians, Persians, Greeks, Romans, Byzantines, Arabs, Mamluks, Ottomans and French. Although often conquered, Lebanon was never subdued, and the Lebanese take pride in their rebellions against despotic and repressive rulers as they strived to gain independence and freedom.

There are archeological remains of thousands of years of human history along Lebanon's coast and inside the heavily forested hinterland. During the Greek, Roman and Byzantine periods, Phoenicia's cities were economically and intellectually active, though they flourished mainly under the Pax Romana, during which the inhabitants of the principal Phoenician metropolises (Byblos, Sidon, and Tyre) were granted Roman citizenship. Trade and maritime activities continued to flourish for several centuries.

Lebanon's enchanting landscape has attracted many different peoples, and its dense wilderness has acted as a shelter for those fleeing war and persecution in nearby lands. Following the collapse of the Ottoman Empire after WWI, the League of Nations handed over the area now known as Lebanon to France. Under the French mandate, the Lebanese began calling for their independence and in 1926 drew up a constitution that granted equal political power to the country's various religious groups.

However, since its independence in 1943, Lebanon has been racked by political turmoil. Several uprisings broke out in the 1940s and 1950s, and it wasn't until the 1960s that Lebanon was able to enjoy a brief period of relative calm during which it attracted tourists and investors. But the cycle of violence started again in 1970, leading to full-blown civil war in 1975 that wreaked immense devastation until hostilities calmed in 1990. With the end of the war came a period of reconstruction, and Beirut rose again from its ashes.

Map of Lebanon

MEDITERRANEAN SEA

- El arida
- Tell Haned
- Machta Hassan
- Al Abde
- Halba
- Andakat
- Qoubiat
- Hadchit
- Rahbe
- Ain Yaakoub
- Fnaidek
- **TRIPOLI**
- Kfar Hdou
- Zghorta
- Sir
- **HERMEL**
- Bkaa Safrine
- Qaa
- Anfe
- Chekka
- Bechmezzin
- Miziara
- **EHDEN**
- Amioun
- Kosba
- **BCHARRE**
- Ras Baalbeck
- Msaileh
- Bziza
- Jdaide
- **Batroun**
- Jrane
- Hadeth Al Jebe
- Hasroun
- **THE CEDARS**
- Garzouz
- Douma
- Ainata
- Tannourine
- Niha
- Laboue
- Kfoun
- Laklouk
- Deir El Ahmar
- Aarsal
- **BYBLOS**
- Ain Bayada
- Aaqoura
- El Yammoune
- Quartaba
- Chlifa
- Knaisse
- *Nahr Ibrahim*
- Afqa
- El Bouar
- Yahchouche
- Kfour
- Ghabale
- **Tabarja**
- Ghazir
- Mayrouba
- Achkout
- **Maameltein**
- Harissa
- Hrajel
- **BAALBECK**
- **Jounieh**
- Feytroun
- **JEITA**
- Reifoun
- Kfar Debian
- Faraya
- Zouk Mikael
- Ajaltoun
- Baskinta
- **Nahr El Kalb**
- Antelias
- Bikfaya
- Bhaness
- Dhour Chouer
- Sannine
- **BEIRUT**
- Jdaide
- Baabdat
- Antoura
- Fanar
- Broumana
- Salima
- Ablah
- Baabda
- Beit Mery
- Kornayel
- Rayak
- Ras El Meten
- Falougha
- Jdita
- Hemmana
- **ZAHLE**
- Choueifat
- **ALEY**
- Kaifoun
- Bhamdoun
- Dahr El Baidar
- Baissour
- Sofar
- Qob Elias
- Chartoun
- Ain Zhalta
- Chtoura
- Mejdel Anjar
- Masanaa
- **Damour**
- **BEITEDDINE**
- El Khiara
- Deir El Kamar
- Kefraiya
- Mdoukha
- Barja
- Baaqline
- Moukhtara
- Jeb Jennine
- Chehim
- Gharife
- Niha
- Joun
- Saghbine
- Yannta
- **SIDON**
- Roume
- **JEZZINE**
- Machgara
- Rachaia
- Kannarite
- Kfar Houne
- *Nahr Zahrani*
- Jbaa
- Adloun
- Douair
- Helalye
- Kfar Ez Zahat
- *Nahr El Litani*
- *Nahr El Hasbani*
- Nabatiye
- Marjayoun
- Hasbaiya
- Kfar Tibnite
- Chebaa
- *Nahr EL Litani*
- Beaufort
- Khiam
- Srifa
- Deir Mimas
- **TYRE**
- Maarake
- Taybe
- Bzouriye
- Kantara
- Aadaisse
- **QANA**
- Houla
- Tibnine
- Bent Jebail
- Naqoura
- Ein Ebel

Nahr El Bared
Nahr Abou Ali
Nahr EL Aassi

Beirut
Lebanon

beirut

Beirut - Zaitoune Bay

Aerial view of Beirut

modern beirut

Beirut survived a decade and a half of conflict, earning it the title "the city that would never die." Despite the chaos and destruction in Beirut during the war, the city was rebuilt as a modern, glittery twenty-first century capital. During reconstruction, several archeological excavations led by the General Directorate of Antiquity revealed priceless artifacts from the Phoenician, Roman, Byzantine, Persian and Ottoman periods.

The pearl of the Middle East is now once again home to thriving trade, banking and financial sectors, and is also famous for its nightlife, adored by locals and tourists alike. Restaurants, coffee shops, cinemas, theaters and shopping malls buzz with locals and tourists all day - and most of the night, too. The city's hotels are full of visitors eager to see the new Beirut throughout the year.

beirut

American University of Beirut Campus

Beirut Downtown

Business area in Achrafieh

Altar of the Saint George Maronite Cathedral

Aerial view of the neighboring churches and mosque – Downtown Beirut

beirut

Sursock museum

Internal view of the El Amine mosque's domes

Beirut - Zaitoune Bay

beirut

General view of the corniche and the pigeon grottos

Various Summer sports activities

13

Beirut nightlife

Lebanese cuisine

beirut

SkyBar Beirut – one of the trendiest open air bars in Lebanon

Beirut sparkling in splendor

Statue representing Lebanese emigrants

the corniche

Beirut's Corniche is a charming seaside promenade that stretches from the Central Business District in downtown Beirut to the towering Pigeon, or Raouché, Rocks, offering uninterrupted views of the glittering Mediterranean. Visitors can watch as fishermen reel in their catches and locals take a dip in the sea. The Corniche is dotted with restaurants and cafes, though one can enjoy refreshments from vendors who sell coffee, corn on the cob and various baked goods from their carts.

Just opposite the Beirut promontory, the famous Pigeon Rocks jut out of the sea like two sentinels protecting the shore. The rocks were formed during an earthquake, and the waves shaped their arches over the millennia. Visitors can take a boat ride to the base of Raouché and explore the small grottoes dotting the rocks.

El Raouché – Pigeon grottos

beirut

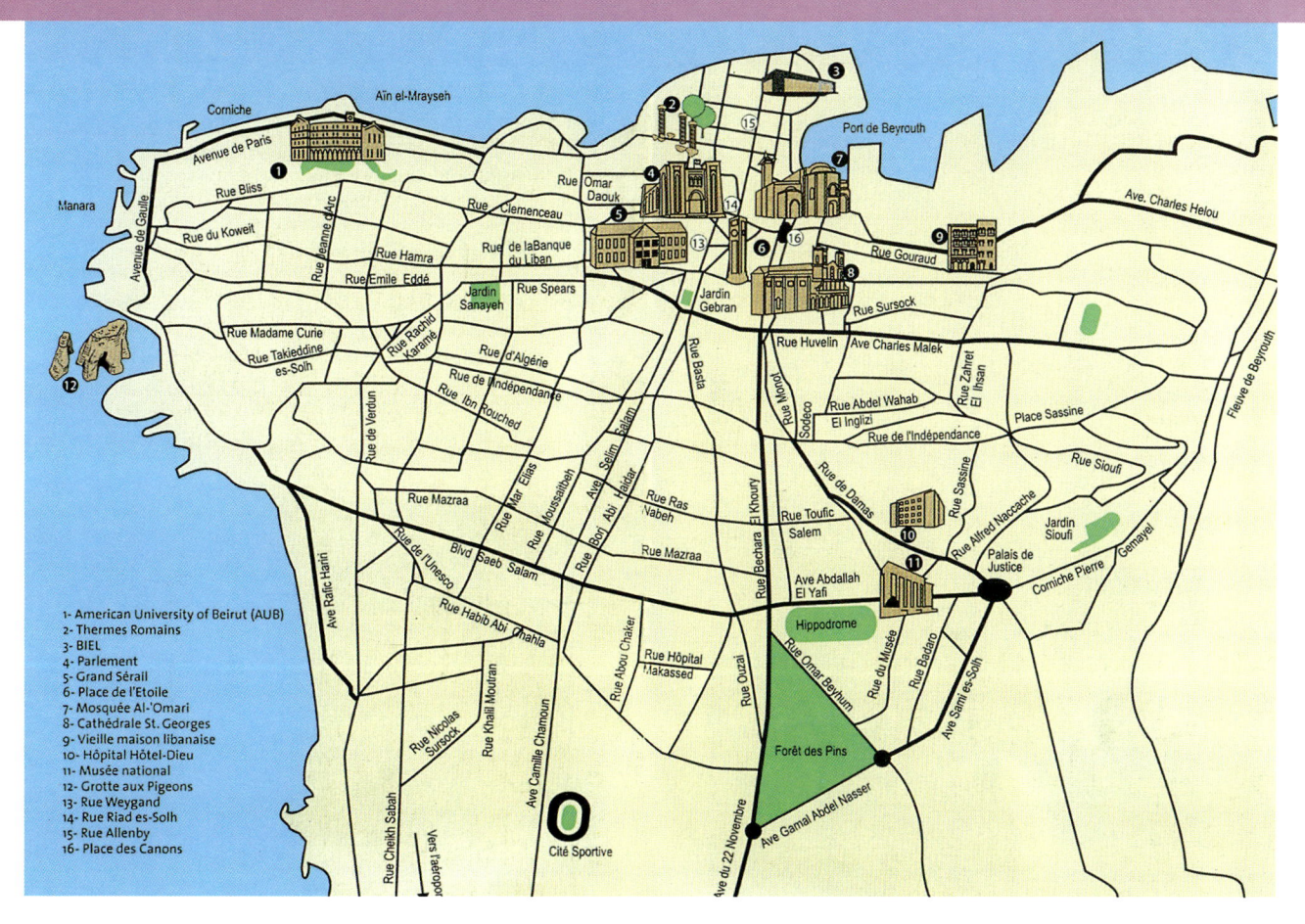

1- American University of Beirut (AUB)
2- Thermes Romains
3- BIEL
4- Parlement
5- Grand Sérail
6- Place de l'Etoile
7- Mosquée Al-'Omari
8- Cathédrale St. Georges
9- Vieille maison libanaise
10- Hôpital Hôtel-Dieu
11- Musée national
12- Grotte aux Pigeons
13- Rue Weygand
14- Rue Riad es-Solh
15- Rue Allenby
16- Place des Canons

the archeological excavations

Ruins from the Canaanite-Phoenician, Roman and Byzantine periods that were excavated before the war benefitted from a good cleanup once the conflict ended. Now the Roman baths behind Banks Street, the Roman columns west of St. George's Cathedral and the Canaanite-Phoenician wall facing the Beirut port area have been restored. The ruins of the famous Roman law school - destroyed during an earthquake in 551 A.D. - are still being excavated.

Beirut is a difficult city to excavate for several reasons. For one, ruins from different periods lie on top of one another, beneath areas that have been continuously inhabited. Building projects throughout the centuries have destroyed much of the city's heritage, and the political instability that has racked the country has postponed excavations and attempts at preservation. However, the complete reconstruction of Beirut's Central Business District offered archeologists a chance to work in the area. The work done in the area can be considered among the largest urban archaeology projects in the world.

The excavations revealed relics dating back to the Neolithic period (the end of the fourth millennium B.C.), when the city was a Canaanite seaport. Archaeological evidence indicates that people in Beirut - like its coastal sister cities of Tyre, Sidon and Byblos - made contact with the Pharaohs of Egypt (2100-1200 B.C.); a stone sphinx was found in 1926, when Beirut's municipality building was under construction.

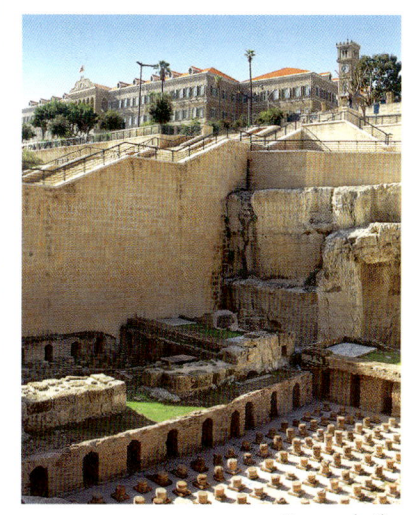

Roman baths   Roman columns

17

Tyrian sarcophagus (2nd century)

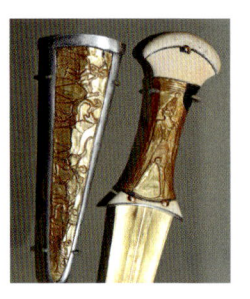

Phoenician figurines

the national museum

The National Museum of Beirut is home to priceless treasures from throughout Lebanon's rich history. The two-story museum is home to mosaics, steles, stone pieces and sarcophagi, some of which are monumental in size. It also exhibits fine artwork such as pottery, jewelry and glass from across the ages.

Since it first opened its doors in May 1943, the museum has conserved, restored and documented its collections, which it makes available for scholars, students and tourists. Since the 1960s, the museum has been one of Lebanon's most important cultural institutions. Its priceless collections were protected, and large objects such as the sarcophagi were molded into concrete when hostilities broke out in 1975. In 1991, the General Directorate of Antiquities decided to repair, restore, conduct inventory and update the museum's collections. With the help of generous public and private funds, the museum re-opened in 1999.

Among the main sarcophagi is the Sarcophagus of Ahiram king of Byblos, renowned for its Phoenician inscriptions. It witnesses the oldest document engraved with 20 of the 22 letters of the Phoenician alphabet. In archeological terms, this sarcophagus constitutes a priceless treasure.

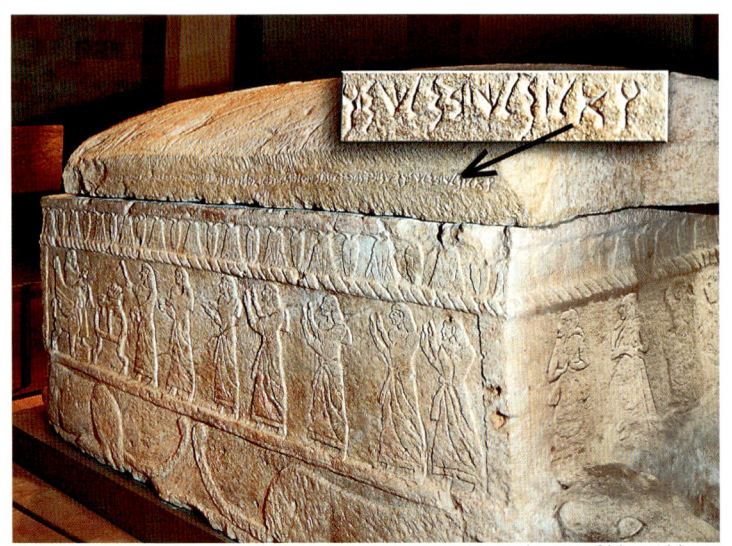

Sarcophagus of king Ahiram

beirut

Robert Mouawad Private Museum

Housed in the Palace of late Henri Pharaon, this private museum is located in the heart of Beirut. The mansion is of neo-gothic architecture with an Arab-Islamic style interior. It has been since its construction as a private mansion by Henri Pharaon in 1911 a reflection of the intellectual dimension of its owner.

Gathering a large collection of art works, books and manuscripts, this palace-museum is an association of the various cultures that dwelled Lebanon, from the Phoenicians, to the Greeks, Romans, Byzantines and Arabs.

Once you come to visit the palace, it indulges you in the pleasure of discovery of its charming precious collections.

All of these treasures would have been lost if it weren't the generous concern of Robert Mouawad, the renowned jeweler who invested much in preserving this cultural and artistic heritage of Lebanon. The palace undertook a seven-years detailed restoration as the current owner insisted on reviving the authentic value of the past.

The museum gathers currently treasures of Phoenician statues, Greek and Roman steles, Byzantine capitals, Syrian sculpted stones, marble and painted wood, books and manuscripts not to forget that Robert Mouawad added to this wealth his personal private collection of jewels, clocks, watches, porcelain and icons.

The museum is a "must-see" destination to discover its wealth and treasures.

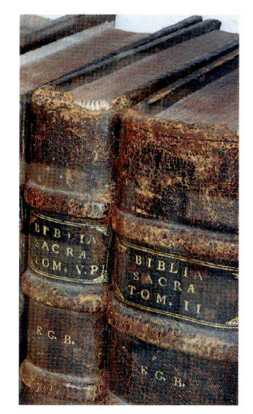

This table witnessed the draft of the new Lebanese flag in 1943

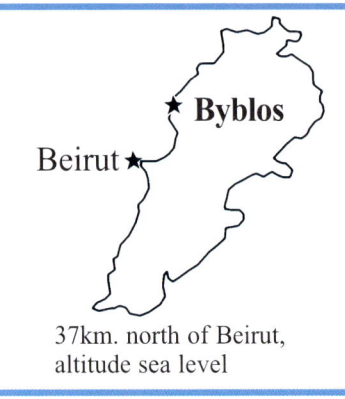

Byblos

37km. north of Beirut, altitude sea level

byblos

The Phoenician historian Philon of Byblos credited the foundation of his hometown seven thousand years ago to the god "El." Byblos was first known as "Gubla" or "Gebal," and it wasn't until after 1200 B.C. that the Greeks gave it the name "Byblos," which means "papyrus" in Greek, as the city was an important center in the papyrus trade. It was originally, however, a little fishing village, as is shown by remains of the Neolithic mono-cellular huts, weapons and tools that have been excavated in the city.

Around 3000 B.C. a massive urban expansion in Canaanite Byblos occurred as sea trade developed rapidly and the city was transformed into an important timber-shipping center for the eastern Mediterranean. The pharaohs would buy wood from cedars and other trees for shipbuilding, tomb construction and funerary rituals. In return, they sent papyrus, gold and linen. This led to a period of prosperity, wealth and intense commercial activity for the city.

Centuries later, around 2000 B.C., Amorite tribes conquered Lebanon's coastal regions and set fire to Byblos. They later rebuilt and settled in the city, and renewed ties with Egypt. These "sea peoples," who came from the northern regions of the Mediterranean, helped the city flourish again. Around the same time, scribes in Byblos developed a phonetic script that was the earliest form of the Phoenician alphabet found on the sarcophagus of Ahiram, King of Byblos.

During the Hellenistic period and the Roman one after it, between 64 B.C. and 395 A.D., Byblos' residents adopted Greek customs and culture. Romans built large temples, baths and other public buildings, which remained during the Byzantine domination. But the beginning of Arab rule in 637 A.D. marked the start of a slow decline in Byblos' importance.

It was French writer Ernest Renan who rediscovered the site of Byblos while surveying the area in the late nineteenth century. Excavations were undertaken from 1921 to 1924 by Pierre Montet, a French Egyptologist, who confirmed the existence of trade relations between Byblos and ancient Egypt. Maurice Dunand continued the excavations and undertook several campaigns between 1925 and 1975.

Excavations have uncovered monumental ruins that now stand right next to modern buildings. The castle, in the north of the city, towers over the Temple of Baalat Gebal (The Lady of Byblos), the L-shaped Temple, the Temple of the Obelisks (which was moved by archeologists to its present location), as well as the Roman Theater, the old royal tombs and the city's fortified walls.

The Temple of the "Obelisks"

byblos

SITE PLAN OF BYBLOS RUINS

1. SITE ENTRANCE
2. CRUSADER CASRLE
3. NORTHERN FORTIFICATIONS
4. NORTHEREN QUARTIER
5. ROYAL NECROPOLIS
6. ROMAN THEATRE
7. ROMAN COLLONADE STREET
8. TEMPLE OF "BAALAT GUBAL"
9. PREHISTORIC QUARTIER
10. "TOWER" TEMPLE AND EARLY BRONZE AGE DWELLINGS
11. FOUNDATION OF PREHISTORIC
12. THE KING SPRING
13. "L" SHAPED TEMPLE
14. TEMPLE OF "OBELISKS"
15. NORTHEAST GATE
16. PERSIAN CASTLE
17. ROMAN NYMPHEUM

Two men playing the trictrac in Byblos souk

byblos

saint john's church

The ancient cathedral of Geblat is a Romanesque building with three apses. It was built by the Crusaders in the twelfth century at the northern end of the city. The church roof is formed of a small dome and holds the bell structure consisting of four medieval columns topped by a mini cupola. The church is dedicated to Saint John Marcus.

The columns and castle of Byblos

the crusaders' castle

Like in Tripoli, the Crusaders occupied the Fatimid fortification over which they constructed a fortress in the twelfth century with Roman building stones. The castle is a strong structure that has five towers encircling a courtyard. A dungeon was later added to the fortress. The castle towers over the area, revealing its strategic importance as a watchtower and guard post at the edge of the city.

byblos

byblos today

Byblos today is a modern, thriving town, a mixture of sophistication and tradition. The old harbor is sheltered from the sea by a rocky headland, home to the annual Byblos International Festival of music and artistic performances. Nearby are the excavated remains of the ancient city, the Crusaders' castle and church, and the old trade area. Byblos is also home to a pedestrian souk, where visitors can meander from modernity to antiquity in a few hundred meters.

The pedestrian souk

byblos

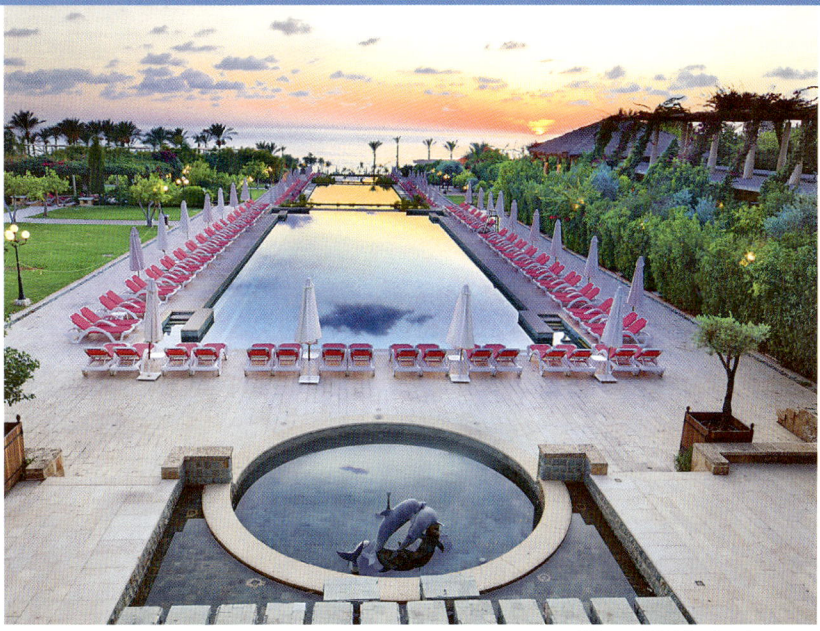

View of Edde Sands resort

Byblos pedestrian souk by night

After long being a modest city, Byblos largely expanded during the 1975-1990 war, as commercial activities moved from conflict-torn Beirut to surrounding cities. These activities also drew people residing in the mountainous region of Jbeil, who decided to settle down in the coastal city. Byblos' main draws are its archeological gems, though it is also a commercial and banking center. It also hosts a number of restaurants, cafes and pubs.

Outside of the city, in Jbeil, another tourist attraction is the village of Hakel, where fossils of prehistoric fish and sea animals are preserved in the rocks.

Hakel fossils

byblos

40km. south east of Beirut, altitude 900m. 3000ft.

beiteddine

The Beiteddine palace

The "Mecharrabieh"

beiteddine

The cool room of the hammam

The Beiteddine Palace is the best example of early nineteenth-century Lebanese architecture. It was built over a thirty-five-year period, from 1804 to 1840, under the rule of Emir Bechir Chehab II (1767-1850), who inherited the land from the Maan dynasty. The emir had decided to move his seat from Deir el-Qamar and construct his own palace in Beiteddine, where he lived with his family until he was forced into exile in 1840 by the Ottomans. The palace complex was transformed into a government residence used by Turkish authorities. After WWI, due to its strategic location, the palace was occupied by the French, who used it for administrative purposes.

In 1934, the Beiteddine Palace was declared a historic monument, and the General Directorate of Antiquities restored it to its original splendor. Following Lebanon's independence in 1943, the palace became the summer residence of the president. Today, Beiteddine hosts a museum that contains artifacts dating back to the nineteenth century and mosaics moved from the archeological site in Jiyeh. With its rambling gardens, charming architecture and extravagant indoor décor, Beiteddine is one of Lebanon's major tourist attractions.

The palace is also the location of the Beiteddine Festival, in which Lebanese and foreign artists and dance troops perform each summer.

The palace water fountain

The main entrance of "Dar El Harim"

beiteddine

Inner courtyard of the palace

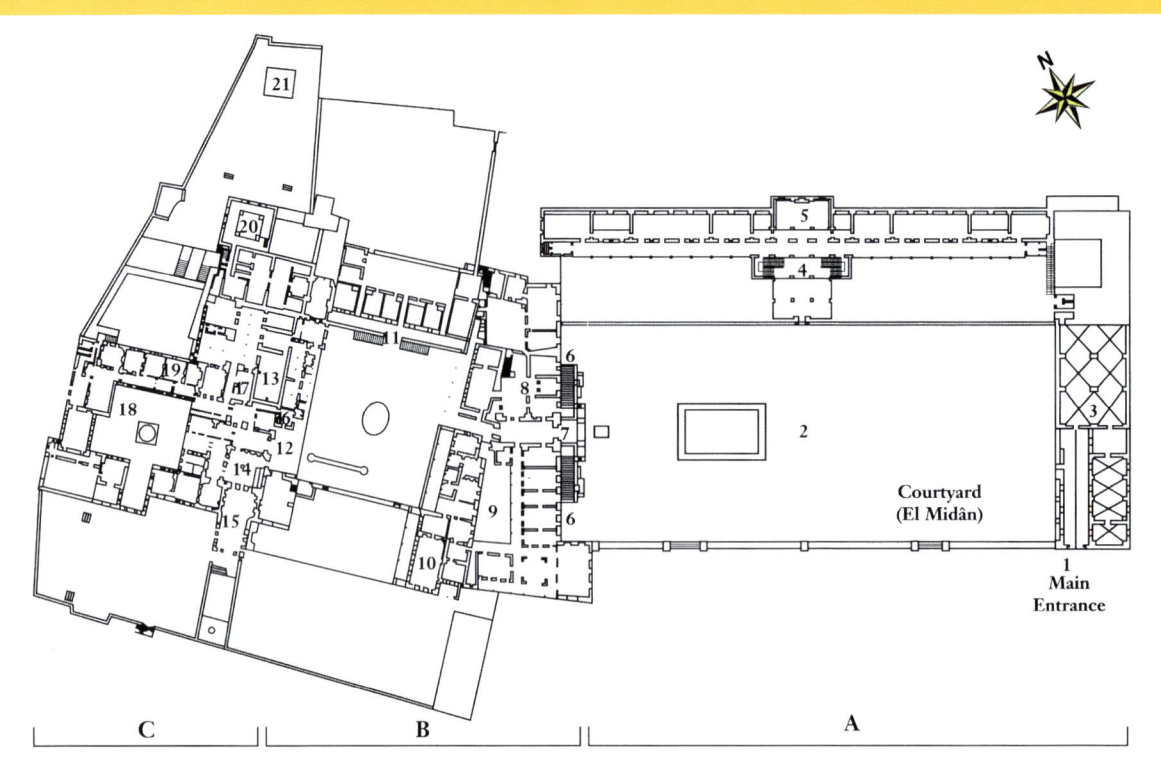

1. Main entrance
2. Outer courtyard
3. Museum
4. Guest wing
5. Ethnographic collections
6. Main staircase
7. Entrance hall
8. Apartments of the Hamadeh Sheikhs
9. Elegant courtyard
10. Boutros Karami's rooms
11. Dar al Kataba
12. The harem wing
13. Upper harem
14. Room of the column
15. Reception hall
16. Lamartine's room
17. Mahkamat
18. Liwan
19. Kitchens
20. Baths
21. Tomb of Sitt Chams

A general view of the palace

beiteddine

the palace of emir amin

Each of Emir Bechir's three sons had his own palace in the Beiteddine area. The Palace of Emir Qassim is presently in ruins and is located on a promontory facing the great palace. Emir Khalil's palace is currently the seat of the local administration and the Serail of Beiteddine. Emir Amin's palace, perched on a hill overlooking the Beiteddine Palace, was beautifully restored by the Ministry of Tourism and converted into a luxury hotel.

moussa castle

Located in the lush mountains of the Chouf, between Deir el-Qamar and Beiteddine, Moussa Castle is the creation of a man who believed that nothing is impossible. The owner of the castle, Moussa el-Maamari, did not let his modest origins thwart the realization of his childhood dream: to build a medieval-style castle for himself. In the 1950s and 1960s, Maamari worked at construction sites in Sidon and in Beiteddine, which allowed him to save up enough money to buy a plot of land, the first step of an unlikely project that lasted nearly thirty-five years. Each and every stone of the castle was carefully cut and engraved by Maamari, who tried to reconstitute scenes of the daily life of Lebanese throughout history.

Visitors have to cross a bridge over a ditch to reach the castle. Once inside, they can climb a spiral staircase to the first floor, where Maamari used life-size dolls to recreate a scene from his childhood in which his teacher punished him for drawing sketches of castles in his notebook.

A vast space is devoted to a display of around three thousand pieces of ancient weapons and artillery that were used in all the major battles in the area from prehistory until the twentieth century. A succession of narrow passages leads from one treasure to another and ultimately takes visitors to an Arab-style salon, where they can enjoy a cup of fresh-ground coffee to the sound of traditional Lebanese music.

Daily life scenes

"Akhwat Shanay" visiting Emir Bechir

beiteddine

Palace of Sheikh Hussein Hamadeh al-Kabir

baaqline

Baaqline is a mountain village founded in the twelfth century by the Maan emirs. Located a few kilometers south of Beiteddine, Baaqline served as the capital of the Maan kingdom until the early seventeenth century, when Emir Fakhreddine II moved to Deir el-Qamar due to a shortage of water in the area. Today, Baaqline is the seat of the Druze sect's religious leader.

The town's Grand Serail, the main administrative building, dates to before WWII and has been restored and transformed into a public library. The palace of Sheikh Hussein Hamadeh, built in 1591, is located at the center of the village. Several Druze religious buildings from the eighteenth and nineteenth centuries - including khalwats, or holy meeting places, and a maqam, or tomb - also sit in the area.

Baaqline is famous for its embroidery, and the lush valley in which it sits draws outdoor enthusiasts, who can hike a twelve kilometer footpath leading to the Berket el-Sabbahin swimming hole.

Palace northwest wing

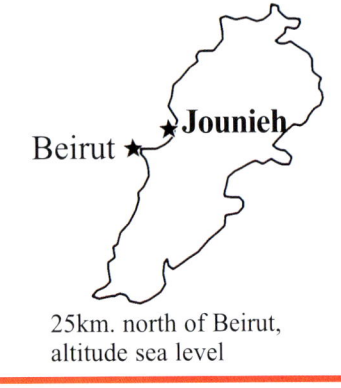

Beirut ★ ★**Jounieh**

25km. north of Beirut,
altitude sea level

jounieh

Jounieh the pearl of the Mediterranean

Summer sunset

An ancient city with a modern twist, Jounieh is located just twenty-five kilometers north of Beirut. Jounieh has kept the charm of the past alive with its old stone souk area, which has recently undergone a complete restoration and hosts a flurry of outdoor cafes, restaurants, boutiques, artisan shops, banks, supermarkets and hotels.
At sunset, the city's daytime charm turns into nighttime glow, as restaurants and nightclubs come alive from the old bayside road in Jounieh northward to Maameltein. The glimmering city overlooks the famous Casino Du Liban, recently restored to its former splendor. The casino - with its numerous bars and restaurants, theater and Salle des Ambassadeurs - is filled with locals and tourists all week long.
Though Jounieh is a popular destination throughout the year, in the summer its annual festival held in the pedestrian souk is a special attraction.
Another famous, but more subdued, site in Jounieh is the Our Lady of Lebanon statue on the Harissa mountaintop. Below in Sarba lays the Greek Catholic Sanctuary of Saint-Sauveur, built on the ruins of a Roman temple dedicated to Serapis.

Cathedral of Saints Peter and Paul neighboring the Basilica of Our Lady of Lebanon, both overlooking the bay of Jounieh

jounieh

Casino du Liban, Jounieh's jewel

85km. east north of Beirut,
altitude 1170m. 3839ft.

baalbeck

A view of the temples of Jupiter and Bacchus

Baalbeck, or Heliopolis in Greek, is considered the most important Roman-era archeological site in Lebanon. Located at the junction of two main historic trade roads, it was a central city and wheat warehouse for the region. Its massive Roman temples, built with the tallest-ever-erected columns and largest stones ever cut still stand majestically at the site.

Around the end of the first century B.C., Baalbeck's temples were built over a Phoenician temple, which was revealed during an excavation. Although little is known about daily life in the area during that period, there is evidence that an enclosed court was built around an altar similar to other Semitic places of worship.

When Emperor Constantine converted to Christianity, he drew up the Edict of Milan in 313 A.D., granting liberty of worship to all, and gave Christians the right to perform their rituals openly. By the end of that century, Emperor Theodosius ordered the closure of pagan temples and transformed most of them into churches. In Baalbeck, he ordered the destruction of the altar of the temple of Jupiter and constructed a basilica using the temple's stones.

Since the seventh century, Baalbeck was conquered several times by the Arabs, Umayyads, Abbasids and Fatimids, and did not enjoy a period of calm and prosperity until the Mamluk rule between the thirteenth and sixteenth centuries.

Parts of Baalbeck were destroyed during the earthquakes that have struck the region over the centuries as well as the transformation of its temples into fortifications during the Middle Ages. Baalbeck has since been largely restored thanks to the efforts of German, French and Lebanese archeologists and architects over the past century.

The first survey and restoration was undertaken by the German Archeological Mission in 1898, followed by research and further restoration by French scholars in 1922, and later by the Lebanese General Directorate of Antiquities.

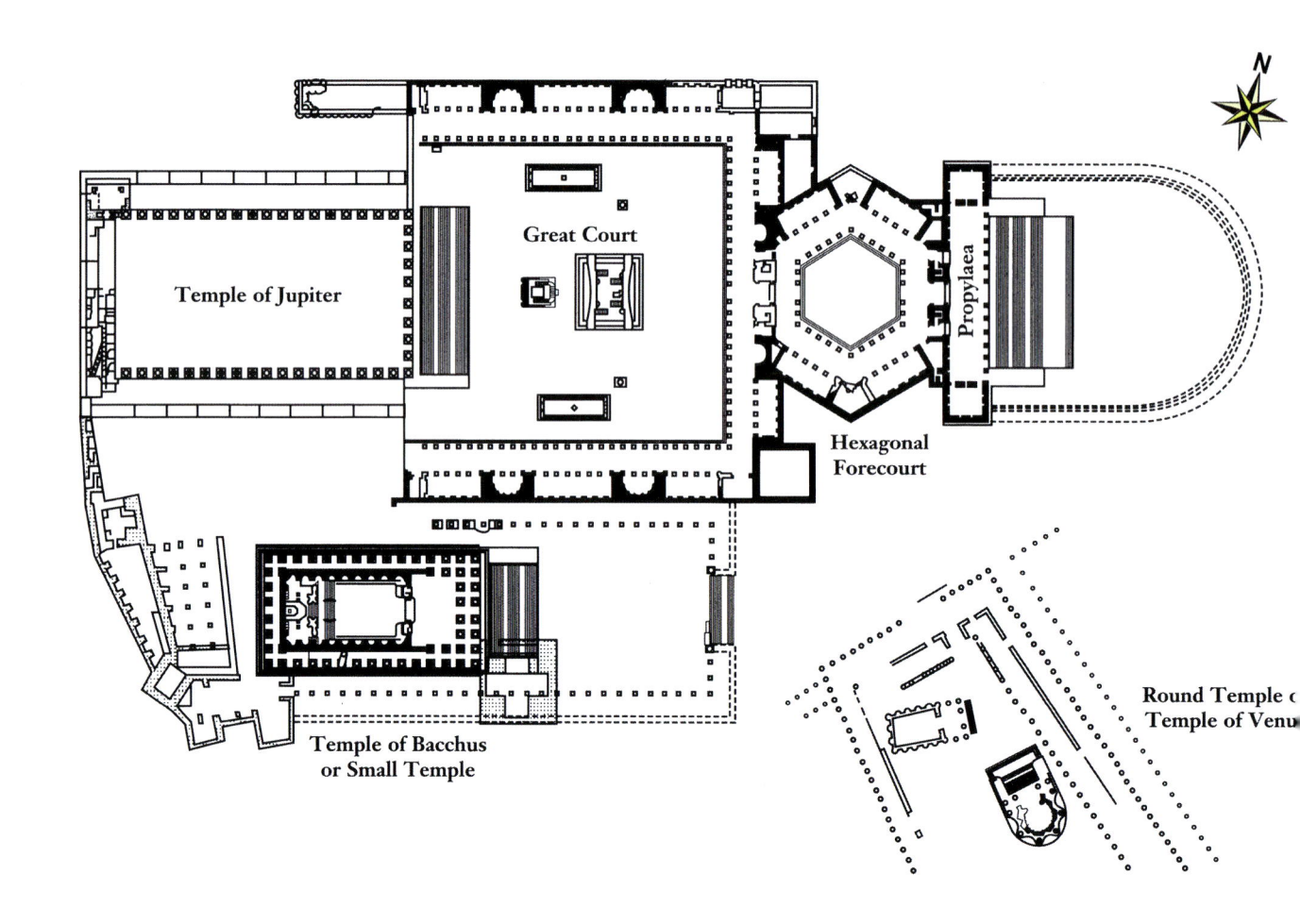

baalbeck

General view of Baalbeck

A visit to Baalbeck starts with the Great Temple complex, which has four sections: the monumental entrance, or Propylaea; the Hexagonal Court; the Great Court; and finally the Temple of Jupiter, where the six famous columns stand.
In 1957, Baalbeck was chosen to be the scene of an international dance, music and drama festival, which was staged at the Roman temples. The annual event was re-established in the 1990s and today draws a large international and local crowd every summer.

the propylaea

"Propylaea" is composed of two Greek words "pro," or before, and "pylos," or portico. Completed in the middle of the third century A.D., it constitutes the monumental entrance to the Temple of Jupiter with a large semicircle of stone benches and a stairway. Originally, the structure of twelve columns was surrounded by two towers that were later transformed into bastions. Now, only a part of the original structure remains. Four majestic columns and the staircase were partially reconstructed by the German mission towards the end of the nineteenth century after being completely destroyed by Arab invaders.

baalbeck

the hexagonal forecourt

The six-sided, fifty-meter-long hexagonal forecourt was built between the Propylaea and the Great Court in the third century A.D. Three entrances lead to the forecourt from the Propylaea, and one can still see the threshold on the edge of the sacred court. The forecourt was the passageway between the sacred court and the common one, where worshippers were sorted by their religious rank, according to local traditions. The forecourt, which was kept closed, was an intermediary space allowing the worshippers to meditate before entering the sanctuary.

Under the rule of Theodosius, a dome was built to cover the hexagonal forecourt, which was transformed into a church dedicated to the Virgin Mary.

Now, the forecourt is no longer covered but is still surrounded by thirty granite columns, which originally supported the entablature and enclosed the portico.

One of the Great Court exedras

the great court

Just beyond the hexagonal forecourt, the Great Court was where the most important religious installations were kept and where sacrifices were carried out. It was surrounded by an elegant portico enclosing four exedras arranged in a semicircle. Almost at the center of the court stood two tower-altars for sacrifices. The great tower, of which little remains, facilitated the access of pilgrims to the tower terrace, so they could see the image of their god nestled in the background of the sacred cella. Both structures, flanked by two water basins, were destroyed at the end of the fourth century and were replaced by a basilica, which was also later destroyed.

baalbeck

General view of the Great Court exedras

View of the Great Court

the temple of jupiter

The first thing visitors see when entering Baalbeck is the six Corinthian columns of the Great Temple that rise twenty-two meters into the sky. They formed part of the peristyle structure that originally consisted of fifty-four columns.

This temple, also known as the Temple of the Sun, was built under Nero's rule and measures eighty-eight meters in length and forty-eight meters wide. It stands on a podium seven meters higher than the court and twenty meters higher than the surrounding lands. The podium is built from three stones weighing one thousand tons each, known as the Trilithon. The podium holds the cella, which shelters the statue of Baal, or Jupiter.

baalbeck

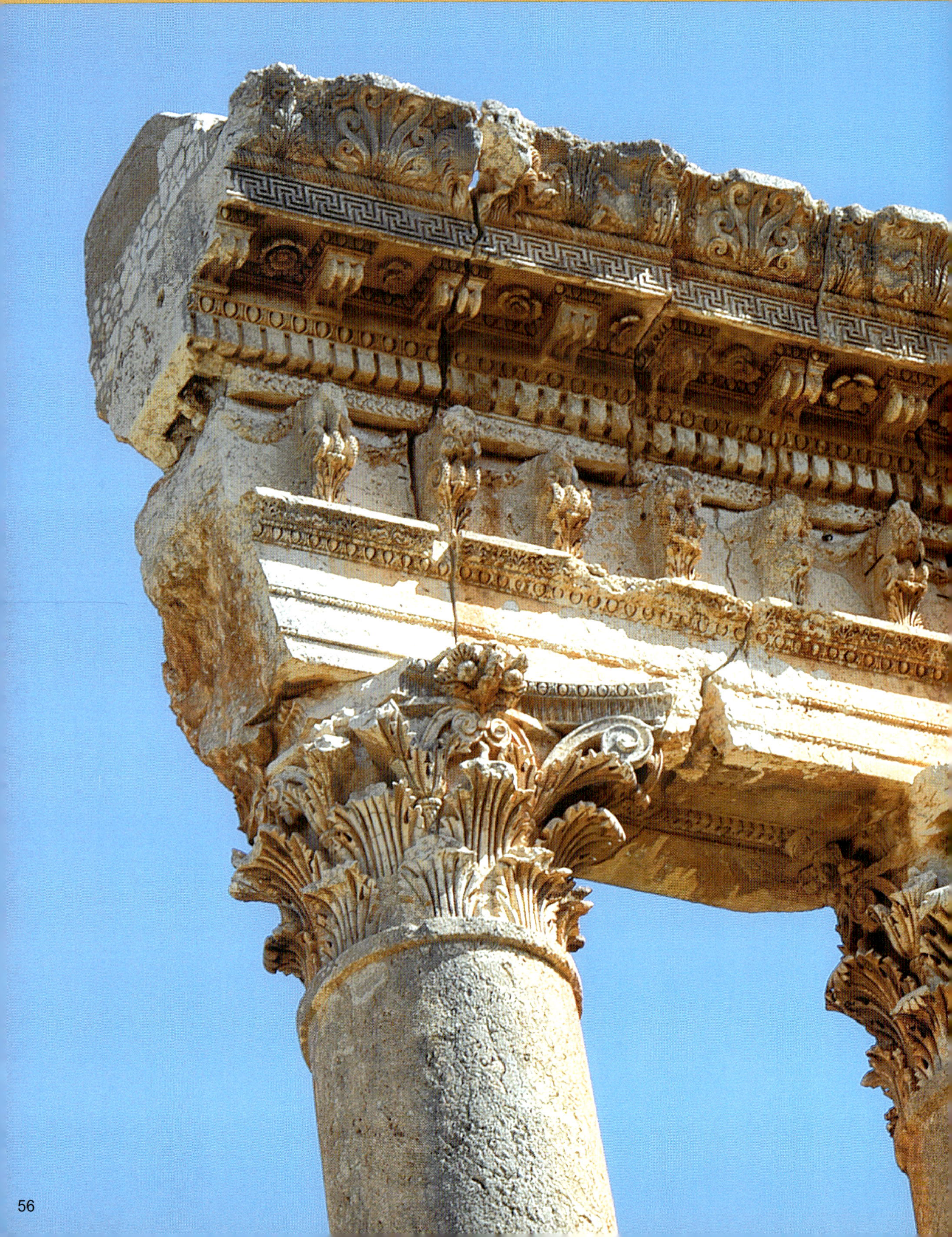

baalbeck

the temple of bacchus

Built next to the Temple of Jupiter, the Temple of Bacchus was constructed during the first half of the second century A.D. It is the best-preserved Roman-era temple in the region. The small temple was consecrated to the young god of Baalbeck, Bacchus, also known as Dionysus or Adon, the god of wine and ecstasy. Bacchus was also the god of growth and fertility, and worshippers prayed to him for eternal life.
At the southwest part of the temple stands the Mamluk Tower, which was the residence of the city governor.

View of the external colonnade of Bacchus Temple

baalbeck

Elaborate and refined decorated ceilings with relief carvings survived the assaults of centuries.

The temple of Bacchus

baalbeck

The Romans built several monumental structures in Baalbeck, among which the baths, the market and the city council room, which were unearthed south of the acropolis. Also to the south of the acropolis sit the remains of several buildings, among which a group of columns rebuilt with their entablatures. These columns probably belonged to the civil Basilica of Baalbeck, although archeologists have not yet determined the type of construction they held. To the south of this site, under Hotel Palmyra, sit the ruins of the theater, or Odeon.

Ruins neighbouring the temples

baalbeck

the temple of venus

Southeast of the acropolis stands the Temple of Venus, built in the third century A.D. Its circular cella is unique in Lebanon. Considering its design, size and orientation toward the Temple of Jupiter, some say it was built for the god of fortune and the goddess Venus.

During the Byzantine period, the temple was dedicated to Saint Barbara, patron saint of Baalbeck to this day. Next to the Temple of Venus sit the remains of an adjacent temple dedicated to the muses.

the museum

The Museum of Baalbeck is situated in the underground tunnels beneath the courtyard of the Temple of Jupiter. It exhibits sculptures, statues and smaller artifacts from the Bronze Age and Hellenistic and Roman periods; but the museum also contains maps, photographs and explanations of the temples.

The museum was opened in 1998 to commemorate the one-hundredth anniversary of Emperor Wilhelm II's visit to Baalbeck. Fascinated by the site's history, the emperor sent archeologists to undertake excavations, which he paid for. Hence, there is a room in the museum dedicated to him. There is also an exhibition of Baalbek's ruins and Bedouin tribes that lived in the area by the German photographer Herman Burckhardt.

baalbeck

the largest stone in the world

Near the town of Baalbeck is the quarry from which the Trilithon stones were cut to be used for the podium of the Temple of Jupiter. The Trilithon stones are the largest hewn stones in the world, each weighing over one thousand tons and measuring 21.5 meters by 4.8 meters by 4.2 meters. According to scholars, more than forty thousand men were needed to move the stones from the quarry to the temple site.

85km. north of Beirut,
altitude sea level

tripoli

St Gilles castle

One of Tripoli's square

Tripoli, or Trablos in Arabic, which sits eighty-five kilometers north of Beirut, is the second-largest city in Lebanon and is called the Capital of the North. Its historical wealth and thriving business climate draw people from across Lebanon, and its ancient history brings tourists to the city.

Medieval buildings - including the Roman and Byzantine baths - are scattered throughout the city. Tailors, jewelers, perfumers, tanners and soap-makers keep shops and work in the souks and khans, which have remained basically the same for five hundred years.

The port city was inhabited by the Phoenicians starting in the ninth century B.C. Under Persian rule, from the sixth to the fourth centuries B.C., Tripoli became the center of a confederation joining the Phoenician city-states of Sidon, Tyre and Arados Island. The city continued to flourish, though in 551 A.D., an earthquake struck the coastal regions of Phoenicia, causing the destruction of Tripoli and other important cities. It wasn't until after 635 A.D. that Tripoli rose again as a commercial and shipbuilding center under the Umayyads, and was developed into a center of learning under the Fatimids.

The Crusaders laid siege to the city in 1109, causing extensive destruction, including that of Tripoli's famous library, the Dar el-'ilm. During the Crusaders' one-hundred-eighty-year rule, the city was the capital of the county of Tripoli.

Later, under Mamluk rule, mosques, baths and khans were built and survive until now. Tripoli maintained its prosperity and commercial importance under four centuries of Ottoman rule (1516-1918), and many buildings from the period are still in use in the city.

tripoli

the citadel or saint gilles castle

The citadel, which is one hundred forty meters long and seventy meters wide, was built on a rock overlooking the city in the twelfth century. What is left of the structure is an octagonal Fatimid fortress, a Crusader church, and some basements, rooms, ramparts and prison cells. It was renovated several times over the centuries, and the Crusaders transformed part of it into a church. The most extensive restoration work on the citadel was done by Mustapha Barbar Agha, the governor of Tripoli, at the beginning of the nineteenth century.

el mina

The el-Mina region is the closest area to the sea near Tripoli. El-Mina, which means harbor, used to be surrounded by orange plantations, though it is now a busy wharf built on the ruins of ancient Tripoli.

To the north stands Bourj es-Sbah, or the Tower of the Lions, a military building erected by Emir Julbân to defend the city against the Turks in the mid-fifteenth century. At the tower's entrance stands a stupendous portico decorated with black and white striped stones, with several rooms and a terrace that have a view of the harbor. Further to the west sit the ruins of a second tower, Bourj Ras el-Nahr, or Tower of the Riverhead.

Tower of the lions

tripoli

Khan Al-Khayyatin

the khans

The khans, which are inns built around a courtyard that can be used as a marketplace, are an important part of everyday life in Tripoli. Among the most important khans in Tripoli is Khan el-Khayyatin, or the Tailors' Khan, which is one of the oldest in the city, dating to the fourteenth century. It was built on the remains of a Byzantine and Crusader monument in the center of the city. The restored structure consists of a long passageway lined with tall arches. To the west sits a granite column mounted by a slab of marble engraved with Corinthian-style letters.

Another important khan is Khan el-Misriyyîn, or khan of the Egyptians, which was built at the beginning of the fourteenth century. It is a traditional two-story structure with arched doorways and an open central courtyard with a fountain in the middle. It is now being used as a warehouse.

One can also visit Khan ed-Dahab, or the Jewelry Khan, which is located at the entrance of the liveliest part of the city, and Khan el-Saboun, or the Soap Khan, which was originally built as a military barracks.

Khan Ad-Dahab

Khan Al-Saboun

Khan Al-Misriyyîn

88km. south of Beirut,
altitude sea level

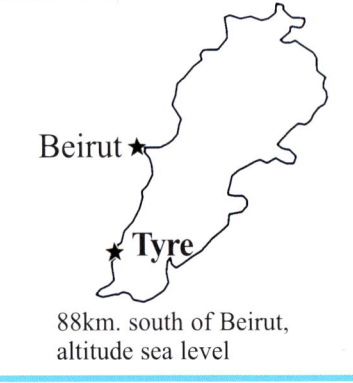

tyre

"El Bass" ruins

73

Phoenician Tyre was one of the most important cities in antiquity and competed with nearby Sidon for commercial influence.

The city, originally called Melkart, grew wealthy from trade with its colonies and from the shipbuilding and purple-dyed textile industries it harbored. It was the sacred city of the Phoenicians and had two parts, one on the mainland and one on an adjacent island.

The Phoenician expansion started around 814 B.C. with the foundation of Carthage in North Africa by traders from Tyre, in addition to the establishment of colonies across the Mediterranean and Atlantic. Much of the city was constructed around 960 B.C. by King Hiram, who enlarged and beautified it, and was admired by conquerors, among whom Babylonian King Nebuchadnezzar and Alexander the Great.

In 333 B.C., Alexander the Great grew determined to conquer this strategic coastal base to defeat the Persian armies. The Tyrians' dislike of the Persians led them to welcome Alexander as a ruler, without, however, allowing him to enter their sacred city. Alexander laid siege to the city for seven months and ordered a causeway to be built to reach the island city. He attacked and burned the island, killing six thousand of its inhabitants and forcing the others to flee.

Nonetheless, with Alexander's successors, Tyre regained its cultural and trade standing and continued to mint its own silver coins. The Romans built many important monuments in the city, including an aqueduct, an archway and a hippodrome.

The city continued to prosper even after being overtaken by Islamic armies in 634 and through the Abbaside decline, during which Tyre acquired some independence.

Tyre also holds an important place in Christianity, as Christ visited the city, and it was mentioned in the New Testament. The Archbishop of Tyre was the prelate of all the bishops in Phoenicia.

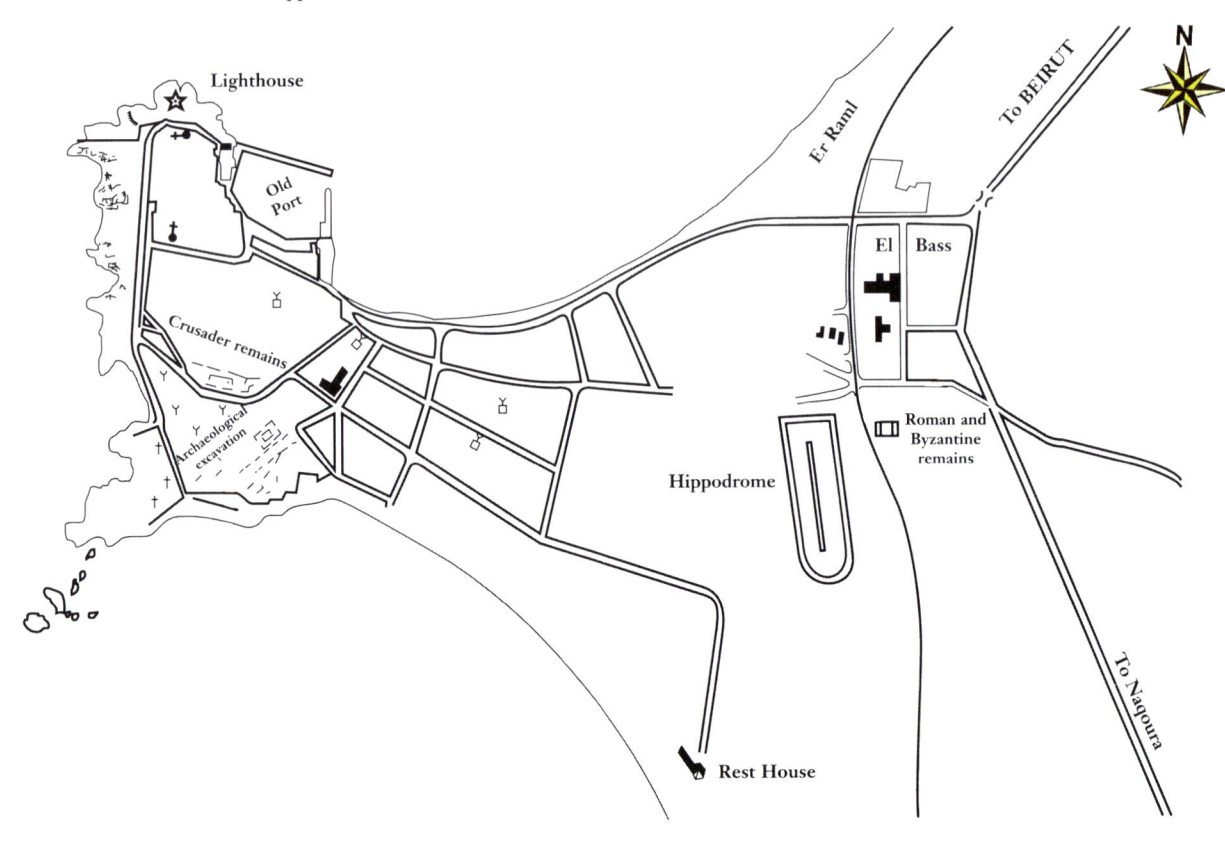

The hippodrome

tyre

tyre necropolis

In the area known as el-Bass sits the Tyre necropolis alongside the Roman road that led to the city. The necropolis dates back to the Roman and Byzantine periods, between the second and sixth centuries A.D., and has a significant diversity of tombs. Tyre's necropolis is considered among the largest and richest in the world.
Several marble sarcophagi were found there, and scholars assume they were brought from Greece or Asia Minor. Other sarcophagi have inscriptions on them revealing the names and professions of the deceased.

the arch of triumph

Important monuments were erected in Tyre during the second century B.C., such as the Arch of Triumph, constructed during the Severus dynasty in the second century B.C., a period that is considered the golden age of the Roman Empire. The people of Tyre built the arch in honor of Emperor Severus Septimus, who helped the city establish colonies.

Located at the eastern entrance of the city, the arch is twenty meters high and is constructed of sandstone and plastered with lime to protect it from falling. The arch used to have three entrances, though only the central one remains today. Two towers were erected at the sides, and the northern tower floor was paved with a mosaic, but the southern tower was made of cubic calcareous stones. The earthquake that struck Lebanon in 551 A.D. destroyed the arch, though the General Directorate of Antiquities was able to rebuild the central part of it.

tyre

the hippodrome

Tyre's hippodrome was built in the second century B.C. and is among the world's largest and well-preserved Roman hippodromes. It is four hundred eighty meters long and one hundred sixty meters wide and could seat around thirty thousand spectators. It hosted many events, the most popular of which would have been chariot races, in which drivers would make seven rounds around the "spina," composed of two rectangular mosaic basins and centered by an obelisk.

tyre

The city ruins

tyre

the baths

The Roman baths are situated alongside the main avenue above the ancient southern port. They cover an area seventy meters long and thirty-nine meters wide. The baths - frequented by people from all ranks of society, even athletes - consisted of elegantly decorated rooms, and had both hot and cold water pools and saunas. Today, one can still see the ruins of the large basins that collected the water needed to operate the impressive facility.

the market

The market was the center of economic and daily life on the island city of Tyre and stood not far from the Egyptian Port. It was a large rectangular area surrounded by columns. The merchants used to display their merchandise, conduct negotiations and do deals in the markets. The markets were also a place for gatherings and entertainment during the Roman period.

the mosaic

The mosaic is an architectural element that was widely used during the Roman and Byzantine periods. There are ancient mosaics across Tyre, such as the one in the Basilica of Tyre and the one that paved the road alongside the Roman baths and gymnasium. The mosaic road was surrounded by two rows of green marble columns, characteristic of the splendor of Tyre around the third century A.D.

tyre

glass factory

Glass was first invented by Tyrian merchants who discovered how to make it when, by chance, they mixed nitrate with water and sand. The Tyrians worked on developing the glass-making technique and began making pots, vases and cups from clear and colored glass around the first century A.D.

boatbuilding

The Phoenicians, the era's most successful sailors, had great experience in constructing boats and ports. Thanks to their flourishing trade with their neighbors, they developed a full industry around shipping. Phoenician boats appear on Egyptian monuments dating to 1400 B.C.

Phoenicians used to construct their boats in a half-moon shape, with two large oars as rudders and a single square sail. Under the Assyrians, the style of their trading vessels and battleships changed, giving way to boats with a high stern, a sharp and pointed ram in front, and double deck.

Tyrians have preserved the tradition of shipbuilding, and the Barbour family still makes both fishing boats and leisure yachts.

Tyre Today

Tyre has a covered market worth exploring, which sits near the busy fishermen's port, referred to as the "Sardinian" port in Phoenician times because it faced north toward Sidon. Tyre's Corniche promenade also gives tourists picturesque views of the city and the sea. Only one medieval tower still stands in a small garden, while a second one can be seen under the lighthouse.

Tyre is also famous for its sandy beach, which is popular with swimmers, sun-worshippers and sea turtles, which lay their eggs at the beach every spring.

For several years, international festivals gathering Arab and Western musicians and performers have been held at Tyre's Hippodrome.

tyre

86

tyre

View from Tyre International Festival

87

58km. east of Beirut,
altitude 950m. 3120ft.

aanjar

Aanjar is a small city founded by Caliph Walid I Ibn Abd al-Malek at the end of the seventh century A.D., and is completely different from any other archaeological site in Lebanon, as it represents only one period, the Umayyad.

Aanjar is also unique in that it is the only historic example of an inland commercial center in Lebanon. It sits in the Beqaa Valley near the point where the Litani River forms a lake.

Aanjar was destroyed in 744 after the defeat of Caliph Ibrahim, son of Caliph Walid I, and it was not until the 1940s that it was excavated. Archaeologists discovered six hundred shops, proving the trading importance of the city at its peak. Excavators also discovered two palaces, a mosque, houses, a structure that was probably a harem, and Turkish baths, known as The Hammams.

Aanjar is among the archeological sites in Lebanon where an annual theater and music festival is held.

aanjar

The Great Palace

The Great Palace is located in the southeastern sector of the city and was the first unearthed landmark during the excavation in 1949. The palace consisted of four distinct buildings surrounding a forty-square-meter courtyard. Only one wall and several arcades in the southern part of the palace have been reconstructed, as well as the six columns holding up the ceiling of the reception hall, where the caliph sat.

To the north of the palace lies a small market overlooking the mosque to the east, which has a rectangular courtyard surrounded by galleries and a prayer room. A fountain for ritual ablutions sits in the center of the mosque's courtyard. The stone settlement is arranged in an ornamental pattern, and the slim columns surrounding the mosque would have let ribbons of light filter into the building.

43km. south of Beirut, altitude sea level

sidon

General view of Sidon

Situated on the southern coast of Lebanon, forty-eight kilometers south of Beirut, Sidon is the third-largest city in the country. It is one of the most famous cities of antiquity, and is the least understood of Lebanon's major metropolises, as relics from its past have been plundered and scattered.

The city was called "Saidoon" by the Phoenicians, which became the modern word "Saida" in Arabic. There is evidence that Sidon has been inhabited since 4000 B.C., when the ancient city was established on a promontory facing an island that sheltered the sailors' fleets from storms.

The city of Sidon flourished under the Phoenicians in the twelfth and tenth centuries B.C. and reached its height under the Persian Empire (550-330 B.C.). Sidon's main industries were glass manufacturing and purple dye, which allowed the city to grow and compete for a place with neighboring Tyre for wealth and commercial importance.

Like other Phoenician city states, Sidon was conquered by a succession of invaders. Sidon's residents rebelled in 351 B.C. against Persian rule, locking themselves inside the city walls and setting fire to their city to prevent the Persians from being able to take it. Over forty thousand people lost their lives. Sidonians, however, did not oppose the incursion of Alexander the Great in 333 B.C., and accepted him as their ruler. Sidon then enjoyed a period of calm, prosperity and relative freedom, and continued to mint its own silver coins under Roman rule. In 551 A.D., when a great earthquake struck the northern shores of Phoenicia and destroyed most of its cities, the Phoenician administration decided to move Beirut's School of Law to Sidon.

The city was occupied by the Muslims in 636, which led to a period of decline until it was besieged and occupied by the future King of Jerusalem, Baldwin, in the twelfth century A.D. Sidon was then taken by the Mamluks, and finally by the Ottomans, who were committed to beautifying the territory. Lebanese Emir Fakhreddine II restored its walls and constructed splendid palaces, baths and gardens in the beginning of the seventeenth century and proclaimed Sidon the capital of his kingdom.

In the mid-nineteenth century, archeological campaigns were launched to retrieve and restore Sidon's lost glory and shed light on the mysterious city's past. Like in its sister towns, excavations were led by French archaeologist Ernest Renan. Further excavations and archeological surveys were later conducted in and around the city, and several monuments were unearthed dating from the Phoenician period, such as the Melkart Temple.

The inland castle of Saint Louis

sidon

sidon's sea castle

Sidon's sea castle was built by the Crusaders in 1228 on the ruins of the Phoenician temple of Melkart. One can still see the Roman columns encased in the castle's walls. The fortress was constructed as a guard tower overlooking the port and the city, and was connected to the mainland by a causeway, which has been restored several times. The west tower of the castle is the best preserved of the site.

sidon's trades and activities

Thanks to its location on the coast, since the city's establishment Sidonians have relied on fishing as a form of commerce and to feed the city's population. Sidon also produces citrus fruits, as the rich soil of the area is fed by irrigation from the el-Zahrani and el-Awwali rivers. The coastal sandy soil is also favorable for palm trees, and the city is famous for its dates, as well as for the sweets local merchants make and stack in pyramids in their shop windows.

sidon

Working fishermen

The modern city of Sidon

98

sidon

The Audi's soap museum in the old city of Sidon.

sidon today

Sidon is a thriving city whose economy continues to rely on fishing and maritime trade. Known as the city of gardens, Sidon is surrounded by citrus and banana plantations, and its northern entrance is lined with palm trees.

Upon approaching Sidon, visitors first see the bustling main street and busy souk full of small and colorful shops. Because of Sidon's thriving economy, its population continues to grow, and new apartment buildings spring up alongside ancient constructions. A football stadium has also been built in the city and hosts games throughout the year.

Restoration projects are currently underway in the city, among which the soap factory, a structure dating to the seventeenth century, which was later transformed into a museum that displays handmade soap.

The football stadium    Bahaa' Eddine Al Hariri Mosque

99

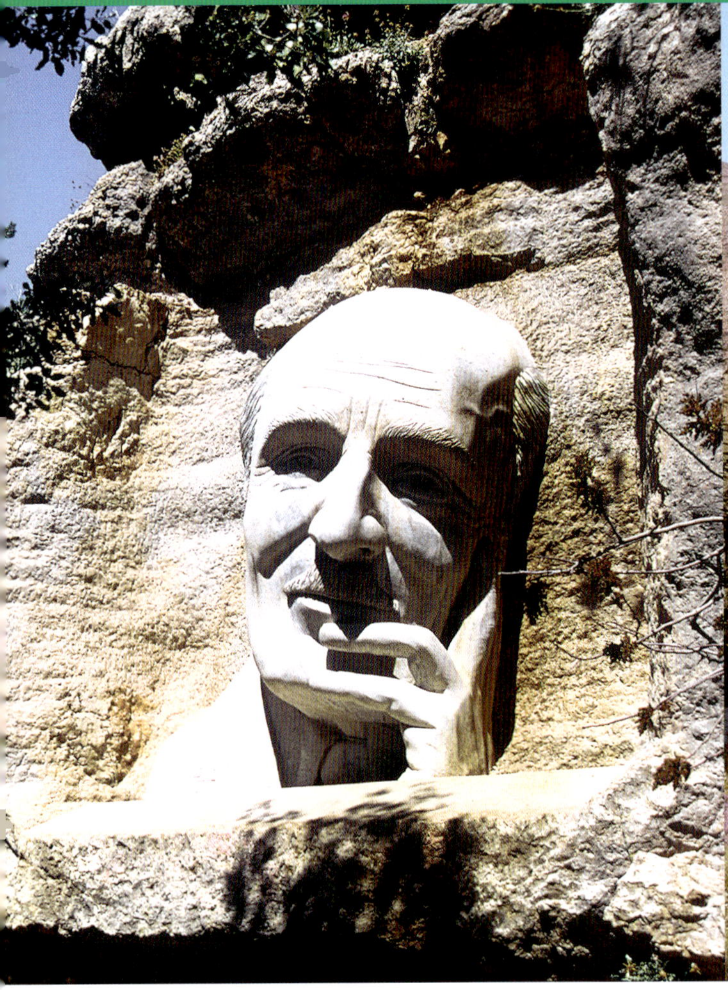

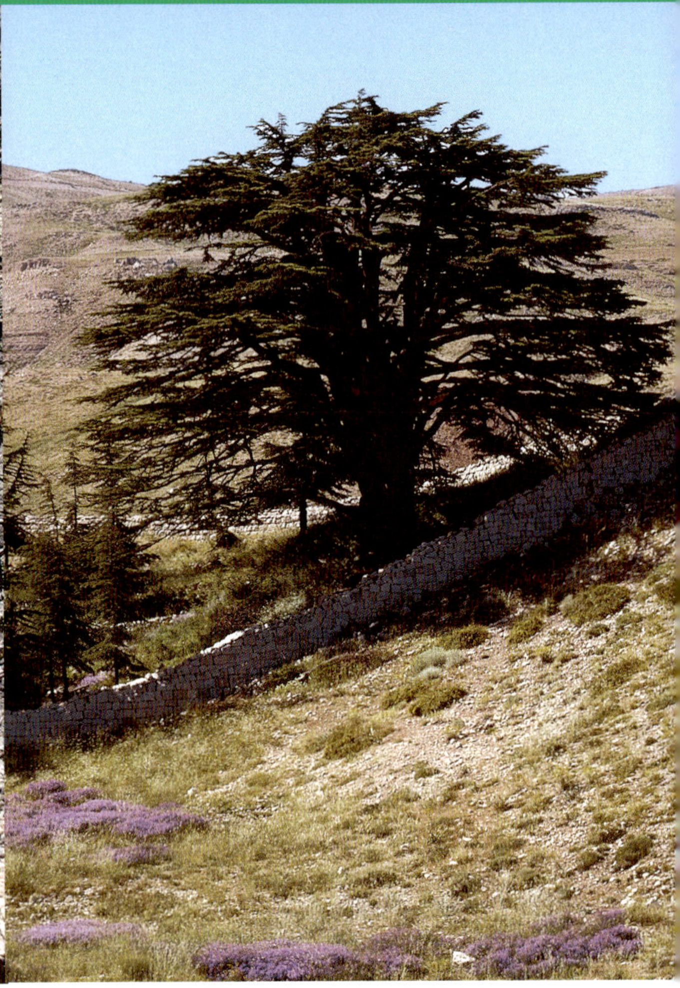

other regions

qadisha valley
126km, east north of Beirut - Altitude 1900m. - 6320ft.

The Qadisha Valley extends over fifty kilometers from Batroun to beyond Becharre, and is crisscrossed by a river of the same name, which flows into the sea between Tripoli and el-Mina. Qadisha is a natural gorge that is protected by mountains, from which numerous waterfalls flow. The valley is the home of the Lebanese Maronite community and is dotted with monasteries dating from the twelfth and thirteenth centuries, built into the rocks and often decorated with splendid frescoes.

Nestled in the scenic and lush valley are the Saint Anthony Monastery - where the first printing press in the Arab world was built and still remains - as well as the Chapel of Our Lady of the Castle, a former outpost for Roman guards northwest of the village of Ehden.

Because of the valley's steep paths, caves and grottoes (among which the Grotto of St. Anthony and the Assy el-Haddath Grotto, where mummies were recently found), it has been used for centuries as a refuge for people fleeing war and persecution in neighboring territories.

The Qadisha Valley is presently on UNESCO's world heritage list.

The first printing press in the Arab world (1610)

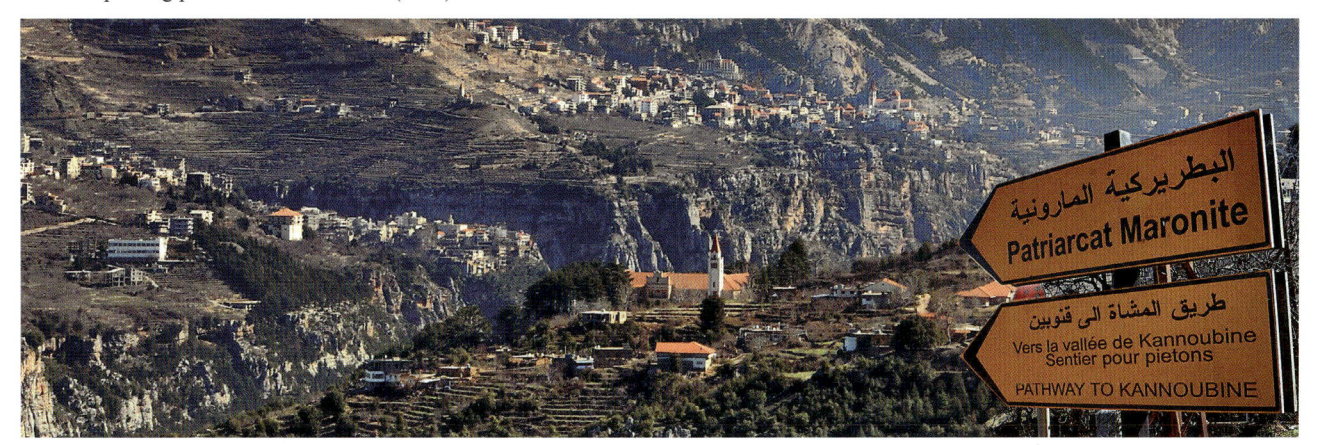

Monastery of Saint Antony Qozhaya

103

Cedars 122km, east north of Beirut - Altitude 2000m. - 6560ft.

Simply known as "The Cedars," this resort area on Lebanon's highest mountain range is one of the most dramatically beautiful spots in the country. Most of Lebanon's ancient cedar trees are found in and around the town of Becharre, the birthplace of Gibran Khalil Gibran. Twelve of the cedars in the forest are over one thousand years old, and around four hundred are more than one hundred years old.

In 1843, under the authority of the Patriarch of Lebanon, a small chapel was built among the trees to protect them, and ceremonies in commemoration of the Transfiguration are celebrated there every year on August 6.

Near Becharre there is a large assortment of hotels, chalets, nightclubs and restaurants. From the village, travellers can take the main road northward to a ski resort and eastward to the Beqaa Valley.

The Cedars is a resort for all seasons. In the summer, the high altitude makes the area a wonderful escape from the humid coast, while in the winter, it offers powdery slopes for skiers.

105

becharre
112km, east north of Beirut - Altitude 1500m. - 4920ft.

Panoramic view of Becharre

The picturesque town of Becharre lies on the road that connects the Cedars to the Qadisha Valley. Becharre, which is located underneath the famous cedar grove, sits at an altitude of fourteen hundred meters and overlooks the Qadisha Valley.

The town is the birthplace of the famous Lebanese poet, painter and philosopher Gibran Khalil Gibran, and there is a museum in town where some of his writings and paintings are exhibited, as well as his tomb.

Gibran's museum

Gibran's house in Becharre

beqaa kafra   115km, east north of Beirut - Altitude 1800m. - 5248ft.

Beqaakafra, the highest inhabited village in Lebanon, lies eighteen hundred meters above sea level, and about five kilometers from the town of Becharre. According to historian Fouad Ephram el-Boustany, Beqaakafra was first inhabited in the tenth century.
Beqaakafra, which means "fertile" in Syriac, is renowned for its natural beauty and charming old stone buildings. Beqaakafra is also known for its religious significance, as it is home to many churches and shrines, and inhabitants wake up in the morning to the sound of church bells and Syriac hymns.
Beqaakafra is also the birthplace of Saint Charbel (1828-1898), and pilgrims flock to the house he was born in to pray, receive blessings and witness the miracles said to occur there. His house is currently under the direction of the Lebanese Maronite Order in which Saint Charbel was a monk. It was transformed into a church and a sanctuary.
Near the village is a grotto named after the Saint, as it is where he used to spend his days praying as a youth.

The house of St Charbel transformed into a church

107

Ehden
Zgharta

114km, east north of Beirut - Altitude 1500m. - 4920ft.

80km, north of Beirut - Altitude 150m. - 492ft.

The Church of Saint Mama, among the oldest Maronite churches in Lebanon

Memorial of Youssef Bey Karam, the Lebanese national figure

Ehden and Zgharta are two separate towns in the north of Lebanon, though many refer to them as one town, as Ehden's inhabitants have been spending winters in Zgharta for centuries to escape the harsh weather.

Zgharta was originally just a few houses and a farm clustered around a tower. The word "Zgharta" is derived from the Syriac term "zegharteh," or barricade, as it sits between Tripoli and the mountains and was thus often hit first during battles in the area. Residents are still proud of their ancestors' historic resistance against attackers.

Currently, Zgharta is the administrative center for the area and is home to a number of schools, hospitals, water and electricity suppliers, and telecommunication hubs. Ehden became a summer resort, as it is rich with water resources, mainly the Mar Sarkis spring, near which sit assorted restaurants and cafés. Ehden is also known for its "midan," or town square, where residents and tourist gather on summer evenings.

batroun   50km. north of Beirut

The phoenician rampart

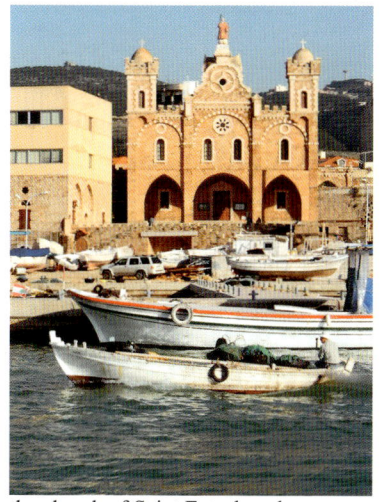

the church of Saint Estephan, known as the "Fishermen's Church"

Living sides of Batroun

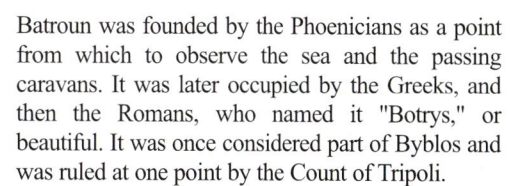

Batroun was founded by the Phoenicians as a point from which to observe the sea and the passing caravans. It was later occupied by the Greeks, and then the Romans, who named it "Botrys," or beautiful. It was once considered part of Byblos and was ruled at one point by the Count of Tripoli.

Today, Batroun is famous for its fisherman's port as well as its rambling vineyards established by the Crusaders.

Batroun has done a good job of conserving monuments from its history. The ruins of the ancient Phoenician port enclosed by a dam are well preserved, as is the Roman Theater to the northeast of the inhabited part of the village, which is surrounded by a private garden. Old religious buildings such as the Orthodox Church of St. George and the Church of Saint Estephan, also known as the "Fishermen's Church," are also well-kept.

Today, Batroun is considered one of the calmest parts of Lebanon, though the village's souk and natural harbor attract visitors from around the country and world. There is also a yearly festival held on August 16 during which Mass is celebrated on a vessel in the harbor, surrounded by smaller boats.

Today, Batroun is witnessing rapid economic and touristic development and growth, and restaurants, cinemas and night clubs are always opening.

annaya
54km east north of Beirut - Altitude 1200m. - 3936ft.

1- Hermitage of Saints Peter and Paul
2- Saint Maron Monastery

Annaya is a mountainous region twelve hundred meters above sea level, and seventeen kilometers from Jbeil. Renowned for its "odor of holiness," the area receives thousands of pilgrims who visit the Saint Maron Annaya Monastery of the Lebanese Maronite Order, which holds the tomb of Saint Charbel.

The construction of the first building in the monastery was completed in 1828, the year of Saint Charbel's birth. Saint Charbel lived as a hermit in the monastery until his death in 1898.

Following the canonization of Saint Charbel in 1977, the monastery was transformed into a sanctuary, and it is said that a great number of miracles have occurred there since. There is also a museum in the monastery that holds replicas of cassocks and utensils used by Saint Charbel.

nahr el kalb   15km. north of Beirut

Nahr el-Kalb (the Dog river) used to be a narrow passage where the mountain slopes down abruptly into the sea, leaving no way through or just narrow passages. It was thought in ancient times that it is worth mentioning the hardships endured by the kings and conquerors who marched through Lebanon over 3,000 years. Therefore, they left inscriptions and steles in the rock above what is now Nahr el-Kalb (Dog River). Over the centuries, other foreign expeditions followed their example, marking their passage through this difficult place by carving their exploits in stone. Today, 17 inscriptions or steles can be visited, all on the south bank except for one on the north bank. Each inscription is numbered, and a stairway leads to those located higher up on the cliff. The single stele on the opposite side of the river was the work of the Babylonian king Nebuchadnezzar II (604-562 BC) who also left two copies of the same inscription in Wadi Brissa near Hermel.

The last inscription was set by the Lebanese Republic commemorating the liberation of South Lebanon on May 24th, 2000.

The old bridge of Nahr El Kalb

111

jeita grotto
22km. north east of Beirut - Altitude 350m - 1148ft.

Few caverns in the world can compete with Jeita Grotto, a Lebanese national symbol. Ranked among the top fourteen most amazing natural sites by the New 7 Wonders of Nature international competition, it is renowned for its astonishing beauty.

The grotto was discovered in 1836 by Reverend William Thompson, an American missionary, who realized how large the cave was from the extent of the echoes of a rifle shot he fired. Visitors can travel by boat on a dreamy five-hundred-meter cruise down the river that runs through the grotto.

The upper galleries, discovered in 1958 by Lebanese speleologists, are made up of cathedral-like vaults that sit beneath the wooded hills of Mount Lebanon. They are renowned for their magnificent stalactites and stalagmites, calciferous curtains and columns sculptured over the millennia by Mother Nature.

Both grottoes have been accommodated to enable tourists safe access without disturbing the majestic natural landscape.

The photos are taken in coordination with Mapas Co.

113

harissa
25km. north east of Beirut - Altitude 700m - 2297ft.

The Basilica of our Lady of Lebanon

Located twenty-five kilometers north of Beirut and at an altitude of six hundred meters, the hill of Harissa is a center point for Catholic communities in Lebanon. On one side of the hill is located the seat of the Maronite Patriarchate, known as Bkerké. On the top of the hill is the Convent of the Greek Catholic Paulist Melkite monks. A few hundred meters higher is the Papal Apostolic See in Lebanon and, neighboring it, the Convent of the Franciscan friars, or the Convent of Charfeh, which is the seat of the Syriac Catholic Patriarchate.

It was at Harissa where Maronite Patriarch Elias Howayek (1899-1931) and Monsignor Carlos Duval, the apostolic delegate in Lebanon, decided to commemorate the fiftieth anniversary of the proclamation of the Immaculate Conception dogma by Pope Pius IX on December 8, 1854 by erecting a statue of the Virgin on the hill. This statue is similar to that of the Blessed Virgin who appeared to Sister Catherine Labouré in 1830. The artist Durenne built it in seven pieces that together weigh fourteen tons. In 1904, the statue was transported to the highest point of the hill and set on a pedestal on top of one hundred steps.

Sts Peter and Paul Melkite Greek Catholic Cathedral

zouk mikaël
14km. north of Beirut - Altitude sea level to 200m - 656ft.

Settled in the beginning of the fourteenth century, Zouk Mikael is nestled on a fertile coastal plain below a mountain, fourteen kilometers north of Beirut. The city is a gathering of houses built around a seventeenth-century souk that has acted for centuries as an important regional marketplace. The souk area was restored after the civil war and is now a pedestrian market mostly featuring cloth creations made by local artisans on looms. Near the souk stands the craftsman's house, where artisans also sell their wares, facing a Roman-style stadium that is the location of an annual music and arts festival. Restaurants and coffee shops dot the area, where visitors can relax and enjoy charming views of the souk and surrounding town.

Zouk Mikael is also known as the city of the seven domes, as it is home to churches and monasteries dating back to the seventeenth and eighteenth centuries.

Thanks to the efforts of its municipality, Zouk Mikael was granted the title "City for Peace 1998-1999 for the Arab countries" by UNESCO. The UNESCO prize sculpture was enlarged and set at the entrance of the Roman stadium.

The UNESCO prize statue enlarged

The amphitheatre

The old souk

kfardebian - ouyoun el simane - faqra

Kfardebian, Faqra and Ouyoun el-Siman sit on a mountaintop in the Kesserwan region. With heavy investment and real-estate development, the area has become the most popular ski resort in Lebanon. The slopes of the area are over twenty-three hundred meters above sea level, and on a clear day at the peak, one can see Syria to the east and the Mediterranean Sea to the west. The village of Faqra, which is part of Kfardebian, is famous for its Roman temple ruins and its natural land bridge between two slopes. Besides skiing, the area is a popular destination for those trying to escape the heat and humidity of the Lebanese coast in the spring and summer. On a warm spring day, one can go swimming along the coast, then head up to the slopes to go skiing in a T-shirt. There are a number of warm-weather outdoor activities to enjoy in Kfardebian, Faqra and Ouyoun el-Siman, such as hiking, cycling and horseback riding. There are stunning panoramic views all year round.

44km. east of Beirut - Altitude from 900m to 2800m - 2952ft to 9186ft.

The white slopes of Ouyoun El Simane

Ruins of the Great Temple of Faqra

Faqra's natural bridge

At Faqra Club, horse riding figures as one of the various summer activities

117

damour

20km. south of Beirut - Altitude sea level to 200m - 656ft.

The Damour plain

Damour sits on the second-largest fertile plain in Lebanon on the coastal road to Sidon. The Damour River flows alongside the city, irrigating the banana and citrus plantations as well as the town's vineyards. Restaurants and cafés are scattered along the riverbanks, allowing visitors to relax in front of the idyllic views.

In the middle of the Damour plain stands the ruins of the famous old silk plant. Tourists can also visit the summer resorts dotting the coastline.

deir el-qamar
35km. south east of Beirut - Altitude 850m - 2788ft.

Deir el-Qamar, which was established in the early fourteenth century, became famous when Emir Fakhreddine II moved his capital city from Baaqline to the town, where he ruled until his death in 1635. The town remained the governor's residence until Emir Bechir Chehab II moved the capital to Beiteddine. The town is centered around the great square, or "midan," which is surrounded by various historic buildings. The water fountain in the middle of the square was added in the nineteenth century and is bordered by the Emir Fakhreddine Mosque. Behind the mosque sit the remains of the nineteenth-century leather-workers' souk, which today houses modern shops.

The town is also the home of the famous palace of Emir Ahmed Chehab, who built it in 1755 for his wife, who in turn sold it to Georges Baz, an important political figure of that period. The palace is now a museum that displays wax figures of famous people in Lebanon's history. Next to the wax museum is the Kharj Barracks, a munitions warehouse built by Fakhreddine II; the Serail of Emir Fakhredine II and that of Emir Youssef Chehab; the Hall of the Column; the Our Lady of the Hill Church; the Mausoleum; and other historic monuments.

sannine
45km. east of Beirut - Altitude 2600m - 8528ft.

Mount Sannine crowned with white

Mikhaël Naimeh, the Philosopher

One of Lebanon's most iconic mountains, Sannine rises abruptly from the coastal plain and reaches an altitude of two-thousand-six-hundred-and-eight meters. The trip up Mount Sannine takes visitors through some of the most beautiful scenery in Lebanon on a winding road that curves around the mountain's slopes with views of gorges and valleys.

Sannine is home to villages perched around its snowy peaks, populated with red-tile-roofed houses that are surrounded by fruit trees and vineyards.

On one slope of Sannine lies Baskinta, the hometown of Mikhail Naimy, a Lebanese writer and best friend of Gibran Khalil Gibran, with whom he founded the Pen Bond in the United States. A statue representing Naimy - also known as the philosopher of Shakhroub, the area where he liked to spend the summer - was sculpted by Assaf Assaf in the rock facing his house.

zahle
52km. east of Beirut - Altitude 1010m - 3312ft.

General view of Zahle

Called the Bride of the Beqaa because of its natural beauty and lovely atmosphere, Zahle is located on the banks of the Bardouni River along the eastern foothills of Mount Sannine in the Beqaa valley.

The city center stretches along both banks of the Bardaouni River, with the older section of town on the upper elevations of the western bank and the shopping district on the eastern bank. At the northern end of town is the Bardaouni River Valley, known as Wadi el-Aarayesh, or Grape Vine Valley, and is the site of Zahle's most famous outdoor restaurants, renowned for their Lebanese cuisine.

Besides its beautiful scenery and culinary standing, Zahle is a business center and acts as the administrative and commercial capital of the Beqaa Valley. It also has an agricultural industry, producing vegetables, fruits, grains and, most importantly, grapes.

The city also has a reputation as an intellectual hub, as there is a long list of writers and poets who hail from Zahle and who have contributed to Lebanon's cultural and scholarly life. Said Akl, Fawzi Maalouf, Shafiq Maalouf, Riad Maalouf and former President of the Republic of Lebanon Elias Hraoui are but a few.

beqaa valley
85km. east of Beirut - Altitude 1000m - 3280ft.

The Qaraoun lake and the dam at its farthest end.

Nestled between the Mount Lebanon and Anti-Lebanon mountain ranges, and traversed by two main rivers, the Orontes and the Litani, the Beqaa Valley is characterized by its ideal climate: warm, dry summers and cool weather during the rest of the year.

This climate is the best for grape growing, and the most famous Lebanese vineyards are located in the Kefraya and Ksara areas of the Beqaa.

During the Roman rule - the remains of which are still visible in the ruins sitting throughout the valley - wheat was the Beqaa's biggest crop. Its fertile soil led the Beqaa to be referred to as the eastern wheat warehouse of the Romans. Even today, the Beqaa's fields produce two abundant harvests every year.

In 1957, the Beqaa Valley hosted the largest lake in Lebanon, when the Qaraoun dam was constructed in the southern part of the valley. This lake has improved the irrigation system to all farms and agricultural lands in the region.

aley
bhamdoun

20km, east of Beirut - Altitude 950m. - 3116ft.
25km, east of Beirut - Altitude 1100m. - 3608ft.

View of Aley

Bhamdoun nestled among pine trees

Until the end of the nineteenth century, Aley and Bhamdoun were just typical Lebanese mountain villages. It wasn't until 1895, when the railroad linking Beirut to Damascus was constructed, that the villages became significant. The railroad facilitated the movement of Beirut's residents out of the city, and they started travelling to Aley and Bhamdoun to spend their summer vacations. The towns' residents therefore developed trades catering to the new tourists, revitalizing the economies and cultures of the towns.

During the civil war, both Aley and Bhamdoun were completely destroyed, though efforts were made to reconstruct the towns in the 1990s with the help of the municipality and the Lebanese government. The towns regained their old charm with the revitalization of restaurants, shops and hotels in the area and with the introduction of sports and leisure activities for tourists to partake in. In this respect, a sculpture symposium was kicked off in 1999, gathering Lebanese and foreign artists, and in 2003, Aley launched a painting symposium. The jewelers' souk, for which Bhamdoun was also famous, has been recently reopened.

broumana
20km, east of Beirut - Altitude 750m. - 2460ft.

baabdat
23km, east of Beirut - Altitude 900m. - 2952ft.

Lebanese traditional house in Broumana

Nestled in a large pine grove in the Metn region, removed from the hustle and bustle of the city, lay the towns of Baabdat and Broumana. Old-style houses with red-tiled roofs sit among the trees, and the plethora of pine trees give the air a cool, fresh scent. Broumana offers visitors a panoramic view unlike any other, as it sits on a hilltop overlooking Beirut and the coast. Both towns, which are studded with buildings dating from the eighteenth and nineteenth centuries, also host a number of luxury restaurants, hotels and summer resorts.

Baabdat town scenery

qana
89km. south of Beirut - Altitude 350m - 1148ft.

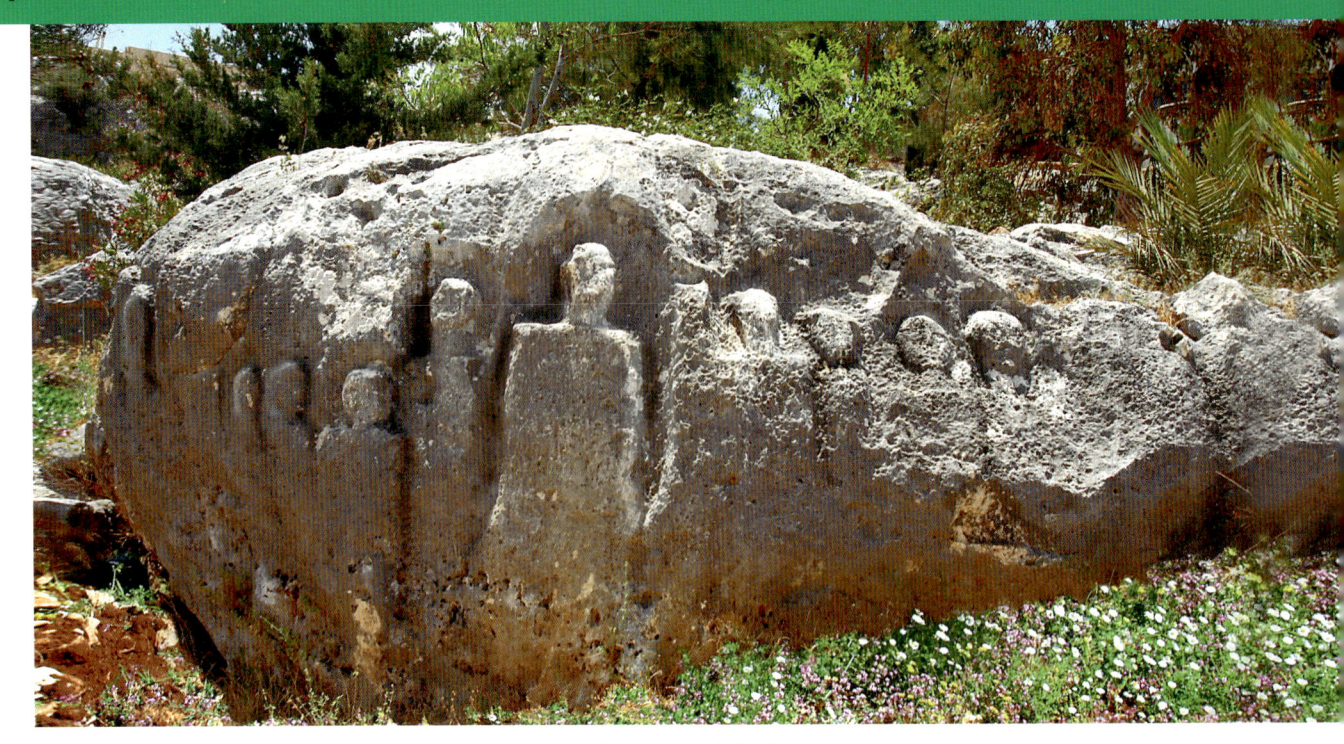

Located around ten kilometers southeast of Tyre, Qana is renowned for its historical and religious significance, as confirmed by Eusebius of Caesarea, the first historian of the Church. Indeed, Qana of Galilee is, according to Eusebius and Saint Jerome, where Jesus Christ performed His first recorded miracle of turning water into wine during the weddings in the village.

Qana was not rediscovered by researchers until the nineteenth century due to its isolated location away from every main road in the area. When they first excavated Qana, archaeologists found several sculptures dating to the beginning of the Christian era, as well as earthenware jars that match Biblical descriptions of the jars Christ used in his first miracle.

Jezzine
70km. east south of Beirut - Altitude 950m - 3116ft.

Jezzine, a historical town and summer resort in South Lebanon, is surrounded by pine forests, vineyards and orchards. Located on a promontory rock, it overlooks the surrounding valleys. From the cliff of Jezzine, one can enjoy a breathtaking view of the surrounding villages scattered across the fertile plain. Ponds, lakes and high waterfalls dot the area.

In ancient times, Jezzine served as a warehouse for Sidon, as it was on the caravan route from the coast to the Chouf, Beqaa Valley and Syria.

Today, the town is internationally known for its handcrafted knives and cutlery made of inlaid mother-of-pearl and bone. Tourists and dignitaries who visit the area have for centuries taken the crafts home as a memento from Lebanon.

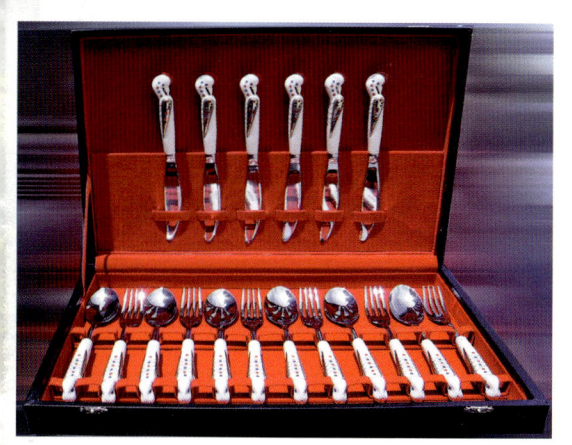

index

Foreword	3	Deir el qamar	119
The History	4	Ehden	108
Aley	124	Faqra	116
Aanjar	88	Harissa	114
Annaya	110	Jeita grotto	112
Baaqline	41	Jezzine	127
Baabdat	125	Jounieh	42
		Kfardebian	116
Baalbeck	46	Map of Lebanon	5
The great court	*52*	Moussa Castle	40
The hexagonal fortcourt	*51*	The palace of Mir Amin	39
The largest stone	*65*	Nahr el Kalb	111
The museum	*64*	Other regions	100
The propylea	*50*	Ouyoun El Siman	116
The temple of bacchus	*58*	Qadisha valley	102
The temple of jupiter	*54*	Qana	126
The temple of venus	*63*	Rashana	109
		Sannine	120
Batroun	109		
Becharre	106	Sidon	92
		Sidon's sea castle	*95*
Beirut	6	*Sidon's trades and activities*	*96*
The corniche	*16*	*Sidon today*	*99*
Modern beirut	*8*		
The national museum	*18*	Tripoli	66
		The citadel or saint gilles castle	*69*
Beiteddine	32	*El mina*	*70*
Beqaa Kafra	107	*The khans*	*71*
Beqaa valley	122		
Broumana	125	Tyre	72
		The necropolis	*75*
Byblos	20	*The arch of triumph*	*76*
Saint John's church	*25*	*The hippodrome*	*78*
The crusader castle	*26*	*The city ruins*	*82*
Byblos today	*28*	*The glass factory*	*83*
Cedars	104	Zahle	121
Damour	118	Zgharta	108

Mosaylaha castle - Batroun